Ten Questions

Principles to Help Heal Our Most Divisive Political Battles

By

Lance Manderville

To Cynthia and Natasha:

At the heart of my heart.

Contents

Introduction

Getting Back to Basics

It is hard to remember a time when our nation seemed less united. The reasons have been discussed, fought over, analyzed, subjected to statistical, academic, political and personal argument, and yet we seem to be sinking further into bitter conflict every day. I admit I've always loved a good debate, and the dinner table when I was growing up was often the place to loudly hash over the daily news and current issues, each of us firm in his or her certainties. Back then it was the Vietnam War, civil rights, the counter culture vs the silent majority, the endless generation gap. Symbolic issues like the length of a man's hair were the source of profound and often enraged disagreement. Okay, so perhaps we *have* been less united at times. After all the United States did have a full on bloody Civil War, so this can't be the worst. But right now, things do seem lousy with dig in your heels conflict, and as engaging as a good lively debate can be, this just doesn't feel fun anymore. And, crucially, it is preventing us, as a nation, from getting things done.

So how can we cut it out? Don't we, as citizens of a single nation, have enough in common to agree on? Maybe one way is to dig deep into our conflicts and try to listen past the many sides, to see if there are principles and ideas we can share, stories we can all find inspiring, perspectives that may not lead to accepting the other side, but at least help us all find a live and let live compromise. After all, we have pending problems, and in the past, as angry as we got, we did find a way to move forward.

This book is an attempt to see past the current battles to some fundamental and pragmatic principles. What this isn't is a set of statistics, or a deep dive into the actual policies and plans. Those things not only have their place, but when the time comes to act it is crucial to look carefully and honestly at the hard facts and relevant history. The truth is though, we already have plenty of hard facts. Unfortunately, our rigid ideologies often lead us to ignore them, or we cherry pick only those facts that bolster our preconceptions.

So instead this is mostly a book of simple stories, analogies that might illuminate the basics. They come from tales many of us already know, or perhaps once knew and forgot: foundational narratives from Western Civ 101, movies we have seen, bits of our history that we haven't focused on in a while. In each case, I think these stories offer powerful insights into our current predicaments.

Do I expect everyone to agree? I sure hope not. Any idea or position is only valuable if it stands the test of honest skepticism. Being proved wrong can be hard to take, but also profoundly valuable: it means our understanding has been expanded. I hope you enjoy these chapters, and even more, I hope they encourage you to get out of your comfort zone, talk things over with those that agree with you, and yes, also those that disagree, plan, and then get things done.

1

Why Should I? Or Why should you for that Matter? The Place of Faith in a Free Nation.

The biblical story of Abraham and his son Isaac chronicles the ultimate test of faith, a matter of life and death of the most terrifying kind. In order to demonstrate to God the depth of his belief, Abraham is called upon not to sacrifice himself - difficult enough - but to kill his beloved son by his own hand. It is hard to imagine a more anguished test. The influence of Abraham's story remains widespread: he is one of the founding patriarchs of the western world's three major religions - Jewish, Christian, Muslim - and remains a touchstone for understanding the elusive nature of faith[1]. What, the tale asks, can God legitimately ask of the faithful, and more to the point, what should the faithful be willing to give. In the story the challenge of faith is essentially private: the test is not spelled out by clergy or community, nor by private reading of a sacred text. God makes the demand

---

[1]   The 19th century Danish philosopher and theologian Soren Kierkegaard's book Fear and Trembling is a wonderful (but dense) description of the difficulties of Abraham's Challenge.

directly to Abraham. Yet acting on the command borders on madness and today we would question the sanity of anyone who claimed he had been asked to do the same. A scientist will tell you that the hallmark of truth is its potential to be proved false, that the measure of a truth lies precisely in the possibility of it being supplanted by another. Faith demands the opposite: in the face of counter evidence - and common sense, and written law - it demands acquiescence. Further, it is one thing to live in accord with faith; quite another to believe the tenets of one's belief should become a law for all. Yet for deep believers, that is essentially the question, for if faith reveals truth, should not one stand for that truth and have it spread outward into the community for the good of all? Perhaps there is a question that could help resolve this dilemma: what of Isaac?

Abraham's story goes basically like this: God instructs Abraham to take his son to the region of Moriah, a three-day journey from his home, and there to sacrifice the boy and make of him a "burnt offering for the Lord." With quiet stoicism Abraham agrees and sets out to fulfill the task. The backstory is that Isaac himself is a miracle child, born of a wife who was too old to be fertile, yet had the child as a promise from God. The boy is a gift, and perhaps Abraham thinks that in a sense all things belong to God. Hard to say, as we hear little of Abraham's inner thoughts. We know he sets out: we know he arrives.

For a modern reader we already know the end: God

will jump in, the boy's sweet young life will be spared. The test is passed. The obvious question is why a test at all for an all-knowing God - surely he knows how it will turn out? The lesson then is for Abraham - and us - that passing the test will result in relief, even joy. As he set out, did Abraham expect he would return to his wife, Sarah, and tell her he had sacrificed their son? Did he expect to live his life in an agony of grief for the boy? Did he wonder if doubt would consume him? What is endlessly compelling, I think, is how the story reaches to the heart of tough questions, of what does faith really mean, and how do we reconcile a just God with the pain of the innocent. On the way up to the chosen place of sacrifice there is a telling moment: Isaac asks his father, since "the fire and the wood are here, where is the lamb?"

A good question indeed. His father assures him that God will provide it. It is hard to imagine the feelings stirring in Abraham at this moment. Here is his son that he dearly loves, and yet he has agreed to sacrifice him with his own hands: he carries the knife with him, an immeasurably heavy burden. In our modern world we are distant from the gore of the slaughterhouse, but Abraham is a rural man: he knows the task will require a steady hand. It will be bloody, and while the first cut may kill, life will not blink out without his son's eyes showing awareness of what has happened. As the story is laid out, this is a test for Abraham. But he is not the only one who will suffer the consequences. One wonders, why should reasons that are good enough for

Abraham also be good enough for Isaac? Shouldn't the boy at least be asked?

We live in a very different world, but that does not mean the dilemmas of the past hold no value for us. At heart this is a story of faith and a test, but also of the basic idea of a reason itself. What is a reason, a good enough reason? A reason to do or not to do, to believe or not believe, to accept a challenge or task or rules from above, or to fight for oneself to be bound to a different task, to live by other rules, to worship, or not, at another altar? When someone insists, this is how to live, these are the rules, this is what matters, what are the reasons that are good enough to make a person say yes and to follow that conception? What are reasons strong enough to obey, to enshrine into a template for doing? And what is a template of doing, if not a law. For Abraham the law was God's word, and therefore the decisive factor in obedience to his own faith. For us rules come in a different shape: the law is made by men and women, open to change over time, built for a large and varied citizenry, with ideas of justice, individual rights, and the common good as measures of the laws' validity.

Our founding fathers were no fools. They were human, they were fallible, but they would not have been able to set in motion what might be the freest and yet most powerful nation in history if they had set us on shaky ground. And one of our proudest freedoms is that of religion. The first amendment states it clearly: "Congress shall make no law respecting an establishment of religion, or prohibiting the free exercise thereof…" What does that mean for us? That your faith is your own choice, that government cannot determine it, nor shall government enshrine any one belief above others. It means Isaac must have a voice. And a choice.

We are a nation of many faiths. And of no faith, counting the atheists among us. When someone decides how to live, they are perfectly in their rights to live by their faith. A meaningful life is something each of has to choose for him or herself, and religion is often the first place to find those answers. The operative word here is chosen: meaning, or faith cannot be dictated to us, and as the price of our freedom, we must accept that others might make other choices, some of which may be disagreeable or even offensive to us.

This is where the public and the private realms are often confused. The passion of one person's belief – and the conviction that the rules he or she lives by are the best for all – may lead us to try to write into public law the rules a group has chosen to live by. But, of course, that is wrong. Wrong if we accept the constitution. Wrong if we accept the very premise of freedom America was founded on. In our world, Abraham can only decide for Abraham. His son must make his own choices.

This is fundamental to what a politician faces, running for office, and if elected, when sworn in. Our elected officials must in effect "take Isaac into account." It is completely out of keeping with our basic principles to enact policies or laws based solely on the tenets of faith. Members of a faith are perfectly in their rights to try to convince others to live by their rules or adopt their way of life. But base the law on it? This gets to the heart of some of our latest debates: abortion, gay rights, stem cells, birth control, all can be fought for or against on religious grounds. Of course, these issues may also be argued about on other grounds entirely: how society is affected, the safety of individuals, possible consequences on children or family structure, the distribution of taxes, and so on. All valid terms of debate. But faith? That is the private realm, the place where you decide for you, and has no excuse for being written into law. And that is the task the politician must accept: that even should he or she live passionately by faith, once elected and the oath of office taken, they must not allow the dictates of that faith to become the foundation for the law. To do otherwise is nothing less than hypocritical.

In the bible Isaac is a pawn in the test between God and Abraham – but here in the US, Isaac gets to choose for himself.

2

Success on a Desert Isle Or, Taxes and Spending

In the movie Cast Away, Tom Hanks plays a modern Robinson Crusoe: his character is a Fed Ex employee named Chuck Noland, whose plane crashes, leaving him stranded on a desert island. Being bright and resourceful, he is able to survive, finding fresh water to drink, making fire, catching fish. He spends four years on the island, and by the end of his stay he is enormously skilled at the survival game, easily providing for his bodily needs, all the while staying basically sane. Yet for all his resourcefulness, there is one thing he just cannot achieve. He never gets rich.

Why not? After all, not only is he the brightest guy on the island, he's the only guy on the island. In the meritocracy game he literally has no competition at all. He works hard, he gives his best, and yes, clearly, he is a success. But wealth? As in money in the bank? As in new clothes, a car, a wristwatch and phone? It doesn't even make sense as a question: none of these things exist on the island, *nor can he ever make them alone*. And that of course is the key: nobody gets rich by him or herself.

If it takes a village to raise a child, it takes a country – and the infrastructure that goes with it – to create the material lifestyle we so easily take for granted.

Imagine you live in a primitive village by the sea. Perhaps it is several thousand years ago, perhaps it is last week, but just one of the places on earth that seem little changed from the past. The inhabitants of the village are few, and primarily make their living from the sea. A smart man will maximize what this living offers: he'll learn the best places and times to fish, how the seasons affect his catch, when the ocean is calm, when it's so unsafe it's best to sit at home and mend his tools. With his skills he will provide well for his family. His wife we imagine will share his resourcefulness, perhaps farming, gathering, salting fish, what have you, but certainly will make a major contribution of her own. She in turn, healthy, well fed and strong, will bear healthy children, and when the time comes the skills their parents perfected will be handed down to them. (I hope no one is offended by these traditional gender roles, but this is a simple village and I'm trying to stay on topic). Like Noland on his island this man is a success, and his savvy has left him materially better off than some of his neighbors. Yet in keeping with the spirit of the community he may share some of his catch with those less fortunate, perhaps villagers who have been injured, or families who have lost their breadwinner. Such generosity is not uncommon, especially in a village where it is likely that everyone knows everyone else, and mutual help is a necessity when the dangers of life may strike even the wisest person. Cooperation is often a crucial cornerstone of such a community's long-term success. It's even possible he had an ancestor who was helped by his neighbors, and thus his very existence is owed to the spirit of giving aid in times of duress. Stop for a minute to look at that: a bit of mutual help is to everyone's benefit. A man at sea who springs a leak can find comfort in the thought that a fellow villager down the coast can be counted on to abandon his own nets to row over to the rescue. This doesn't even address those tasks that really do require many hands to succeed. Isn't it easier to build a new shelter when the whole village turns out together? And when those pesky war-like villagers down the coast come calling, a shared defense really is the only defense. What do we call all these mutual things? Community. And the big house they build together for meetings, or the trees they fell together to build canoes? Not to mention the skills to do all these things, passed down, honed and improved over the generations? This is, in a basic way, infrastructure.

Today it is possible for someone to live in material splendor that would have dazzled an emperor of old. Technology and the division of labor mean your children may be educated by specialists in their respective fields, your health maintained by doctors who spend decades in school, while your home may be filled with wonders like instant heat, instant hot water, clean and safe food and drink and storage to keep it cold and fresh. We have entertainment from giant screens, and hand held devices with more computational power than those on the Apollo lunar module. We have thousands of choices for music, art, movies, a service that will deliver your letters across the country in days for a few quarters, roads that can take you nearly anywhere on the continent, phones that allow us to speak instantly to friends and family around the globe. Does any one of us make all these things for himself? No matter how brilliant, ambitious, hardworking and talented, no one can create these things in isolation. These are the products of a modern society, one with technology and the infrastructure that allows it to function, built over generations, by innovation that rides on prior knowledge and the collective labor of thousands, from the folks sweating in the sun to lay down our roads, to the mineworker scraping out fossil fuels or the precious metals that every phone needs to function to the banker helping a business grow or the scientist with a new cure for cancer. All of us are interdependent, and the wealthiest among us is must still rely on those of us at the bottom of the ladder to do the daily grunt work. This division of labor is what makes the whole shebang roll. Of course, not everyone who works gets the same pay out of it. Some labor takes specialized skills or is more physically demanding - and some of us are just plain willing to work harder or longer, so it is completely logical that we have differences in earnings. Trying to give everyone the same piece of the pie surely devalues effort and skill and is why communism is doomed to fail. Still, think back to our fishing village; not everyone took home the same size catch, but what everyone did have is the same access to the ocean of fish itself. Of course, that kind of clarity of equal opportunity is difficult to achieve in a modern society; accidents of birth color our lives, from the wealth of your parents to your race, sex, looks and the quality of the local schools. We can, and do, try to mitigate this: for example, no decent person would argue that education should only be for the children of the wealthy. That would strike us as not only unfair, but disastrous in the long run for the overall success of our economy. While we can't really see a way to achieve perfectly equal opportunity, surely getting close to that is a laudable goal.

So, first principle: all of us are economically interdependent: everyone plays a role, high or low[2]. We are all better off with a currency that is secure, with schools and roads, with banks and yes with a government that regulates it all to make sure that the bank is a safe place to put that currency, and that the water coming out of the tap is healthy to drink and that

---

2   This is not to say that each of us as an individual is essential. It is just that each role - each job - is an important and valuable part of the economic whole. Sure, somebody else could do your job - but that goes for every job, from CEO to janitor. Those at the top like to put out the idea that their personal skills are irreplaceable, but even a cursory look shows that is untrue. Think - no Steve Jobs, okay, no Apple, but would we still have smartphones? Of course we would.

the schools will do at least an adequate job of making sure the next generation is able to function and work. Infrastructure is not a one shot build it and sit back forever - it is an ongoing process of build, repair, change, evolve. Stability and communal focus are the basic pillars that make this infrastructure work today and allow us to maintain, extend and grow it for tomorrow. The skills that keep the whole thing afloat are so numerous, and so varied, that no one person - or even one family - could hope to do it all. Fair opportunity is that everybody – yes everybody, not just the children of the wealthy – will have a chance to learn and thrive with access to the basic tools that enable them to succeed. Even in the simple fishing village, you have to learn to fish, to handle a boat, to fix a net. Each generation teaches the next, and each generation builds on what came earlier. Our world is more complicated, but the principle is the same. Not only does infrastructure allow our economy to function, changes to it allow the possibility of new opportunities, fueling growth. Take one example: nationwide mail service. We all complain about the post office but think of the huge business opportunities brought about by being able to order goods and have them delivered to one's home. Never mind the roads to deliver it over. Or the road you drive to work on for that matter. Who builds and maintains these basics? Public works? Private industry? A partnership of the two?

On May 10, 1869 a golden spike was tapped into a pre drilled hole by Leland Stanford to commemorate the completion of the first transcontinental railroad. Private industry made buckets of money building that (and plenty of it dishonestly, truth to tell), but it is hard to imagine the project getting off the ground without government help, oversight, planning and yes big giant land grants that helped make the efforts of private industry profitable indeed. The nation wasn't linked coast to coast just because a business said it should be, but because the government stuck its nose in to make it happen. Rural electrification, rural postal service, the interstate highway system, the Brooklyn Bridge, the public school down the road and the internet you can use to look up the history of any of these things, all came about with at least partial government intervention. Like heading to the tap for clean water? Like buying a steak and being pretty sure it's safe to eat? Like expecting that everybody's kids should have a least a shot at getting educated? The private sector has never done these things alone. Never. Yes, private industry can play a big role: hiring a private company through competitive bidding to build a school makes sense. But just sitting around waiting for the private sector to build your local high school is a fool's errand.

Second principle then: the government is not your enemy. Lots of things that we take for granted – like roads, like the thirty-year mortgage, like tested medications that actually work – are the product of government intervention. Many Americans have come to the conclusion that the government should be shrunk to nearly nothing. But that is too broad a point. The question shouldn't be whether or not to make the government smaller or bigger, but rather just how much do we need, *specifically*. Note that last word. When you ask how big government should be, don't think in terms of size, but in terms of what you want it to do and how much does that cost. Government at its best is a tool we all rely on. When a politician sells you on smaller government, ask him or her just what exactly they want to dump. And just how much will it save. And how much it will save you exactly. Same goes for regulation. To say we are over regulating is really to say nothing. Ask just what regulation is inappropriate. Remember, the instruction manual for a jumbo jet is bigger than the one for your bicycle, not out of mean spiritedness, but because it's more complicated and a whole lot more dangerous. Banks, mutual funds, gold mines, all can be messy and dangerous if run wrong (how many gold mines use cyanide to purify the ore? Do you want cyanide running downhill to your drinking water?). The question is not are we over regulating, but what is a sensible regulation that allows business to succeed and yet be safe and transparent for everybody.

What about wealth? All this infrastructure doesn't just make our lives better; it also provides tremendous opportunities to accumulate wealth. Transparency in banking and investing, a stable money supply, places we can park our money, places to borrow money, a stock market for large corporations to raise capital, all these things are the basic tools of wealth. Say you work harder, or smarter, or luckier – you still need to offer a skill or a product, and you need to get paid for it. That means a marketplace, that means consumers, whether individuals or other businesses. It is this flow of labor and skills and money that allows wealth to accumulate, it is the hard worker and the eager buyer that make for economic interactions, and it is the society with a broad range of interactions that most provides the chances for wealth to be gained.

None of this is free, so next question: who pays, and how. Well, that means taxes. Surely no fool alive likes taxes. But we want certain things (I for one do like a road to drive my car on), and somebody's got to pay. So, who should it be?

Look around. Who contributes to our economy? Who contributes more? Who contributes less? Who takes home more money, who less? Is there a perfect correlation between what one contributes and what one earns? Often, yes there is a close relationship: the guy who works overtime makes more. The software engineer who maxes out his credit cards to build a startup might make a killing. Hard work, high risk, these can often be lavishly rewarded, and I think most of us feel that is pretty just. On the other hand, the news is chock full of the opposite: CEO's with golden parachutes running companies into the ground and walking away with millions. Lawyers suing on the drop of a dime with what is nearly extortion. Quick question

– why is money made from money (investments) seen as better than money made from work (income)? Who says it is? Our tax code does. Look around at your neighbors: the teacher who prepares the next generation for work, maybe the next Bill Gates, the next scientist who patents a great drug, or software, or product. The doctors and nurses who help us recover from illness, the plumber who keeps the sink running, the factory worker who builds the cars we drive, and so on to the broad range of jobs, some paid well, some hardly paid at all, yet every role necessary to the functioning of our economy, society and communities. Some of us benefit greatly, some just enough from our economy. Doesn't it seem fair that those who have benefited the most from this economy, that all of us have contributed to, should pay more? No sensible person says the wealthy should be taxed to the point that all the larger gains of their work are eliminated. When someone says taxes should be cut, this is another one of those cases where you might want to know just whose taxes and just how much *specifically*. It isn't really a great bargain if you save a few hundred dollars, while someone else saves tens or hundreds of thousands, especially if that means the roads fall to ruin, or the price of college leaves our children with ruinous debt. History shows if taxes are cut deeply, then we just end up with a greater concentration of wealth in a few hands, while the infrastructure that insures the health of our economy and the fairness of opportunity for everyone and every generation falters.

To wrap up: to make the accumulation of wealth possible, we need an economic, social, and technological infrastructure. To get that we have to build it, generally over generations. Many aspects of that infrastructure literally will not exist without some form of government intervention, whether through direct building, through funding, or through the kind of oversight that makes sure the benefits of this infrastructure are freely available to all. Just as we have benefited from this infrastructure, we have an obligation to keep it going both for all of us today and the next generation tomorrow. Some of us have benefited more than others by our economy, some deservedly so, some perhaps not so much so, but those who have made more can fairly be called upon to give more to our economic upkeep. We all contribute to this in our own way, and as the flow of goods, services, labor and income flows though us, we all are in a real sense job creators and the bedrock of our economy. Progressive taxation is fair and sensible and should be tailored to both the needs of maintaining infrastructure, while still allowing those who contributed more to enjoy the greater rewards that provide such motivation.

And while material goods are certainly worth working for, let's not forget the one thing that Hank's modern Crusoe missed the most: other people.

3

—

(The Smell of) Your Neighbor's Business or the Good Neighbor Approach to the Environment

Have you ever had a noisy neighbor? Or a dirty one, whose lack of cleanliness is not only an eyesore for the block, but borders on a health hazard? Loud parties? Trash piled at the curb? Please keep it down, you beg, it's 3am! But the party goes on. Have they no sense of decency? Where, oh where, is common courtesy?

A frequently voiced lament: society is not so polite anymore, not so civil. Why should we care? After all, looking for courtesy from others is in essence to put a limit on them, to say, no, sorry, but as a neighbor you just *can't* do that. But why not? comes the reply, you're stamping on my lifestyle, limiting my freedom. I like to party, it's my place, who are you to tell me what I can and cannot do on my own property. The fact is, at some point, your neighbors' freedom butts up against yours: they like to party, you like to sleep. They like to pile trash, you like a clean street. It seems like there ought to be common sense solution here. So try this: my neighbor has a right to freedom up until the repercussions of that choice fly over my fence: I too have rights, and one of them is for peace and quiet, cleanliness and health, to sleep without interruption, for me, my family, my neighborhood. Is that fair? Most communities agree, in one way or another, and have gone as far as to have written "quality of life" issues right into the law, even zoning areas so a backyard nightclub doesn't suddenly pop up just over the fence. And this courtesy - to live and let live, is essential to the very definition of a "good neighbor." Let's keep that in mind: the good neighbor. One with courtesy. One who expects the freedom to enjoy their property but recognizes that compromise is often needed if one person's freedom isn't about to damage another's. Now expand that a bit - what if your neighbor's noise, or odor, or waste isn't about a party, but a business?

It starts simply: an entrepreneur lives next door, with a start-up run in his or her garage. Who can complain? A first it's just fine – one woman or man with a little chemistry set and the occasional whiff of something drifting across the yard. But then success hits. Soon the minimal whiff is a constant billow, the smell is a bit foul, maybe your eyes sting a bit, and your poor kid develops a cough, then a wheeze, then a diagnosis of asthma. As if the odor wasn't bad enough. As if the delivery cars all day weren't bad enough. And, by the way, who knows what is in that stuff they're working with. And now isn't that an expansion off the garage, and aren't those employees punching a time clock. And then, at the very least, you start to think: this is *not* a good neighbor.

We have come to the essence of a fair number of our laws. Most of us want to do, well, whatever we want to do. And we want our neighbors to have the same freedom. You deserve the peaceable enjoyment of your home; your neighbor deserves to make a living. Well, you say, that's why we have zoning regulations.

So now you're an environmentalist. What? Clean air, clean water, noise controls - there it is, the essence of the environmental movement. Well, one argues, lets enforce those zoning rules. Reasonable enough, so the business moves down the road a bit, the noise is limited to the commercial center of town. Fair enough. After all, we need businesses, we use and need their products, our communities need a tax base, we all need jobs. This is a meaningful response. There is a line, where the needs of a business bump up against the needs of the people around it. One can and should have a discussion about that line and just where to draw it. But that is not how the argument often plays out: instead we get blanket complaints that any and all regulations are "job killers" and must be gutted, without a fair and honest assessment of the rules themselves. Or, just as silly, a knee jerk reaction that says *everything* needs to be regulated - not in my backyard! - comes the cry.

Perhaps you are old enough to remember the controversy over DDT. In 1939 the Swiss Chemist Paul Herman Müller discovered the insecticidal properties of DDT, and the chemical would prove so effective both in protecting crops, but even more importantly, in helping to manage mosquito populations, that he would go on to win a Nobel prize in 1948 for this discovery. Widespread use of DDT helped wipe out Malaria in a number of areas around the globe, (although its effectiveness dropped over the years due to evolving resistance by the targeted insects). But there was a cost, not imagined at first. In 1962 Rachel Carson's book Silent Spring was published; in it she cataloged the dangers of the widespread use of chemicals such as DDT, a possible carcinogen. Probably the aspect that most galvanized the American public around DDT was its effect on birds, and particularly the Bald Eagle, America's fierce and beautiful symbol. In the wild DDT found its way into fish and birds, and predators that are higher up the food chain - like the Bald Eagle, which is an avid fish eater - found themselves with higher concentrations of the insecticide. Eggshells from effected birds showed "thinning" and the population of Bald Eagles (as well as other birds) declined precipitously. DDT, combined with habitat loss and unregulated hunting, had the birds on the road to extinction in the lower forty-eight states. Our national symbol was nearly wiped out. This became a catalyst for regulation, a fight that took years to resolve. Remember, DDT had proven its effectiveness. Large businesses manufactured the chemical, helping to provide jobs in that industry as well as a good profit. Outlandish claims came from both sides - that Malaria would resurge in the U.S., that crops would be destroyed en masse, while on the other side unproven claims about the carcinogenic qualities of DDT were touted. In the end the chemical was regulated. Today, it is still used around the globe, but as part of a multi-prong approach that seeks to limit overuse (to avoid insects' evolving greater resistance) along with other insecticides, improved health care, and the use of screens and netting.

The details of that fight (from congress to the media) make for fascinating reading even today, and I think both sides would be surprised by what they might find. A pro environmentalist would find a real eye-opener to hear about the human benefits - yes benefits - of an effective measure to control a devastating disease. Someone who believes that environmental regulations are always a pointless drag on the economy might not expect to read how a program that attacks the problem from multiple angles is actually more effective than simple widespread spraying. I think all of us would be cheered about the Bald Eagles resurgence in the lower 48 - our national bird, again successfully breeding on American soil. Looking back on that battle to understand our current ones, how should such a fight be resolved?

Any time there is a conflict, it seems there are a few rules that might help us come to a resolution. The first let's call the rule of skepticism. Quite simply, *everybody's* claims are worthy of doubt. Try to step back - starting with yourself. Do you naturally lean one way or another? Well try not to lean - listen and learn instead. And recognize that different people are vested in different ways - the environmentalist might be overly cautious, sure, but you can bet a businessman is going to push anything that puts money in his pocket[3]. Exaggerated claims are to be expected when people are deeply attached to an outcome, so don't reflexively believe either side.

Next, try to see what the evidence really is. Have tests been done? Have they been repeated by others? Who hired the testers, or funded the research? Few of us are scientists and can deeply analyze a scientific study. That is a natural part of the division of labor, of specialization, that helps make a modern economy run. Instead, consider the money trail. Does their funding really come without strings attached? Is there a large consensus among researchers? Remember, false claims can be a real career killer for a scientist, so there is some pressure to be honest. And one nice thing about science is that any claim made, to be truly "scientific" must be able to be proven false - that is testable. Unfortunately, this means sometimes it is easy to say the evidence is "uncertain" - to cast just enough doubt to make people think they may as well ignore the issue. Keep this in mind though - do you want lead or arsenic in your drinking water? I don't think so. But why not? Because you tested those things yourself? Or because you have *some* trust in the scientific consensus that those elements

---

3   That is assuredly not evil - profit is the job of business, and wealth ethically got is something to be proud of.

are harmful?

None of this is easy. And that is the point - blanket statements like "regulations are just job killers" or "all corporations are evil" are just plain nonsense - each issue deserves its own fair assessment on its own merits. We all have our biases, and politicians probably have the most - they'll often say whatever makes the "base" happy, or a big donor, or most of the time just have a certain ideology of their own, and damn the facts.[4] But let's get back to the good neighbor - the one you want next door, the one you want, if you have any decency, to be. The good neighbor respects those around him or her. Sure, he wants freedom to do as he likes, but he won't just dump on others to make it happen. When, as it happens, your neighbor doesn't really turn out to deserve the title "good" then it seems reasonable to set out a few rules - laws and regulations - to help goodness prevail.

And by the way - it's nice to see those Bald Eagles - our national bird - nesting again on American land.

---

4   I very much mean those on both sides. Remember jobs matter, health matters, it all matters.

4
—

It's Just a Cake isn't it? Gay Marriage and Free Access to the Marketplace.

How do we define an *American* community? A small town in North Dakota that is booming from the fracking industry is going to feel quite a bit different than a Texas one surrounded by oil fields, even though both are economically centered on energy production. A Kansas town bound by acres of wheat fields can't really be the same as one set amid the strawberry farms along the California coast, yet both are growing the food we eat. Never mind comparing the high rises of Manhattan to the car culture of L. A. Endless similar comparisons can be made, from city to country, the heartland to the coasts, all these places that look different from each other, feel different, have their own individual character. Then look within: is your neighbor just like you, does everyone where you live look alike, worship alike, work at the same jobs, vote the same way? Even within the same individual we find an endless array of characteristics, some profoundly meaningful, others really just superficial, so that even how we define ourselves varies by circumstance, whether it be by job, by neighborhood, by race, by faith, and so on, an endless array of factors and roles. Differences abound, an endless catalog of style and yes substance, of opinion and background, race and faith, age and health, gender and orientation. Is the answer then that there is no single answer? And - lacking sameness, are we doomed to a fruitless search for a mythical place, a mythical shared identity, one uniting singular American way to be?

Of course, if we were all alike, would this even be America? Fundamental to our idea of nationhood is the idea of freedom, the right to be who one wants to. The pursuit of happiness doesn't define happiness - only the right to seek it, without reference to a set of defining ideas as to what that entails. In the abstract at least, we celebrate individualism and the right to personal difference, yet in practice those distinctions can lead to conflict. Let's look at something that can keep us apart and then ask - must it?

Recently the Supreme Court ruled on a baker's religious freedom - by, in some ways, dodging the issue. The question at hand was, could the baker refuse to make a cake for a gay wedding? The ruling was very narrow - this time, yes, he could refuse, but because of a technicality about the case and the way the local officials expressed their feelings on matters of faith. The ruling did not say every baker could refuse. So surely this will come up again. What, then is the fair and just answer?

Freedom of religion is a fundamental right in the U.S, written explicitly into the Bill of Rights as part of the

First Amendment. It is clear that the government (at this point both state and federal) has no basis whatsoever in determining the content of someone's belief, or the content of a church's teaching (of course subject to common sense limits). These are matters of faith and are not subject to regulation. This content - the creed - can be argued about, among believers and with those that do not believe, but argue is not the same as rule on with the force of law. The courts have consistently agreed on this. That leaves us with a difficult question: if someone is acting in sincere belief, can that person use that as a reason to be granted an exception to otherwise relevant laws?

The short is answer is yes - but with caveats. The courts - and Americans in general - clearly want to respect the right of believers to live in accord with their faith. Frankly that seems fair, and fits nicely with a goal of maximizing individual freedom, as well as protecting the rights of all our diverse believers in the U.S. The problem, as it often does, lies in the details, and how claiming an exception on the basis of faith can have an effect on others. Remember our first chapter - would we hold Abraham legally blameless as his hand rose to sacrifice Isaac? Not if he had gone through with it. There are limits, and one exceeds them at justifiable legal peril. But it is clear that society - and the law - has a duty to try to accommodate sincere belief. So where to draw the line?

The historical answer to this has been a moving

target. At our nation's founding race based slavery was written into the constitution, and to help protect that horrible institution from being voted out of existence, our founders also wrote in the 3/5 compromise, ensuring that slaves who had no political power themselves would be used to calculate the amount of representation a state would have at the federal level. After the Civil War discrimination against blacks came in the form of many overt laws designed to support segregation. Religious leaders and institutions have historically fought on both sides of this divide, some citing the bible to promote equal rights, while others stating that segregation - and even slavery - are countenanced by God. The sincerity, on each side, of belief in a particular stance, cannot be legally doubted. Can one, on religious grounds, say run a business that refuses to serve or hire African Americans? For decades the answer to that was yes, then the civil rights movement happened. At this point most Americans (but certainly not all) agree that the need for all Americans, regardless of skin color, to have equal access to the basic social, legal, and economic areas of life cannot be denied on the basis of religious grounds.

There seems to be two big takeaway messages here. The first is that the state has an interest in protecting the free exercise of religion. The second is the recognition that denying certain groups access to full economic participation - jobs, services - is not justifiable on religious grounds. There is a legal doctrine that may be seen as a metaphor for why this matters: the concept of common carrier.

Imagine you run a private commuter rail service. Lots of people rely on your service to get from a to b. Heading to work, visiting friends and family, travel - all depend on your service. Not that your service is the only means to get around - there are cars, taxi's, other choices, but your line is the most practical choice. There are times when you might legitimately deny service to someone, even if they need this rail to get to work. Someone who is disruptive, interfering with the driver, harassing other customers - I think most of us would agree those are just causes to kick someone off a train. Now what of race? What if your faith tells you that the mixing of races in public is wrong? Or what of religion - what if your faith tells you that Jews, or Muslims, or Christians should not mix? Are these legitimate reasons to deny service? I think most of us would say no. Free access to public life is one of the basic principles of a fair and just society. The train owner, even though he or she owns those trains outright, can't just deny service on grounds of his or her belief system.

Which brings us to the bakery shop. Gay marriage is now the law of the land. Many religious groups view homosexuality as fundamentally wrong. They have every right to this belief - remember, the law does not allow us to question the content of someone's faith. So how do we reconcile the fair and just access to economic life - jobs, stores, restaurants, - when that means someone will have to give that access in spite of it offending their fairly held faith?

So far much of what we have looked at is fairly abstract - legal doctrine, history, understandings of common carrier. Two good principles – religious freedom vs fair and free access to our shared social and economic life – are now in irreconcilable conflict. Legally, that seems to describe the situation – because respecting one side means the other will have to give. Such questions will always be with us, because being free, we will certainly not always agree. How these things shake out is critically important, but perhaps there will never be a perfect answer, at least in terms of legal decisions. But that is tremendously divisive. Can we recognize the conflict, but look at it a different way? So, instead of the rules, let's look at the people involved. The baker is a man whose faith is profoundly important to him. He is not merely being asked to bake a random cake - but rather for a ceremony that he believes is profoundly wrong.[5]

Now look at our gay couple. I doubt very much that they really want their celebration to turn on forcing

---

5   I have not taken on the issue of gay marriage itself. I would say though, why not allow it? Religious grounds? Remember, it is not religious freedom to force others to live by any one particular creed - that is Theocracy, and surely not a road we as a nation would suddenly like to take (Iran anyone?). What grounds then to deny two consenting adults the right to marry? Scientific? Psychological? Social? None of these realms have any reason to deny that has not been discredited - only custom stands in the way. Let each of us pursue his or her own happiness, with a limit set only how it directly affects others.

someone to bake a cake.[6] As the saying goes - you want food "cooked with love," not by compulsion. Is there a solution that allows us to at least live well with each other? Not if we focus *only* on the rights of each side.

Imagine you are a devout man of faith who believes homosexuality to be profoundly wrong. Now imagine your home is on fire - and the volunteer fireman ready to risk his life to save your family or belongings is gay? Would you let it burn rather than let him into your home? Would he refuse to help if he knew your opinion of his love life? What of jobs - do employers get to reject candidates based on their faith? Could an atheist refuse to hire anyone religious? The list goes on and on, and, I think leads us not to the American ideals of tolerance and mutual respect, but to a splintering of the common space. When we start to limit people's access to that public interaction, we lose our most valuable asset - the American people themselves - and the full participation of each of us. Instead of focusing on the fireman's sexual orientation, consider instead his or her common humanity, the courage to fight a fire, the willingness to do this dangerous job.

Admittedly it is natural to want to interact primarily with people that share one's beliefs. We tend to select out some aspect of ourselves - race, religion, even the simple commonality of going to the same high school, growing

---

6   This of course cuts both ways. Even if you know the Church down the hill preaches a creed you find disturbing, that can't be a reason to deny its members access to any service you in your work life provide.

up in the same area - and then use these as shorthand for identity, thereby finding others "like" us who we associate with. By accepting others who are different than us we are in essence recognizing the validity of their choices. At times that may have the result of undermining the certainty of our own beliefs. If what is different is equally valid, then how can I be sure I'm right? But that is the fair cost of freedom - would you want to live in a nation where only one faith was treated as legitimate, or one political party? Majority or not? If you do, then you don't really accept the very premise of the United States, where each of us gets to decide how best to manage his or her own individual "pursuit of happiness" and no one gets to prevent others from the fair pursuit of their own.

I know this doesn't really answer the question - does the baker have to bake the cake? That is a legal question, and while we have seen that there is a long history of accommodation for religious beliefs, there is also an American principle of maximizing access to the public space for all. The courts have and will continue to decide such cases. Sometimes the baker will be able to opt out – but then the employer will not, nor the hall or tuxedo rental or the honeymoon bed and breakfast. Perfect answers, legally at least, will elude us. That imperfection can tear us apart – but remember your neighbors, different as they are on the surface, still share much with you, and have facets of common humanity – the desire for individually chosen terms of happiness, but also for a shared community, neighbors to trust and work together with, and build a commons of free and open society. Not every slight deserves a lawsuit, but at the same time to coldly deny someone access to the shared economic and social space can be painful and unfair as well. We tend to focus on the differences. But I ask you to go deeper, and consider that what you do to keep this space as open as possible for all, despite our differences, will contribute the most freedom for each of us to be true to who we are in this public realm, for ourselves and our children.

5

Isn't Everyone Better Off? A Pragmatic Approach To Health Care

Imagine this: you just lost your job. You've got bills - who doesn't? Mortgage or Rent. Food on the table. Credit cards. The dentist - never mind the orthodontist. Gas in the car, the car payment itself. Then there's insurance: so many kinds: life, health, car, home. Daunting, to say the least. You might be a tough, can-do sort of person, put a smile on it, crack out the resume the very next day, start the calls. No matter what, there is a lot to worry about, never mind the stress of who are you anyway, if not a breadwinner. But there is one thing you won't have to fear, even if all else goes to hell, even if the bills pill up and the months drag on. What could that be?

School. That's right, sending your kids to school. Sounds silly, but we, as a nation, long ago decided that every child should at least have a shot at an education. Usually we worry (and argue) about that too: are the schools any good, should we vote for charter or vouchers, school choice vs community schools, the unions, and, if you have the money, private as a choice. But the basics - k through twelve - is going to be there even if you haven't a dime in your pocket. I don't think it's a stretch to say all of us - the whole country - are better off for this: an educated populace is a requirement for a successful economy. Most jobs require at least basic levels of literacy, not to mention the complex sorts of work done by engineers, doctors, lawyers, electricians and the myriad of other specialized tasks a modern nation needs to have done in order to prosper. By making basic education universal we help maximize what is arguably our most valuable asset and the cornerstone of our infrastructure: the American people.

How is this paid for? Taxes, often a mix of state, local and federal, with property taxes making up a large share. People with means are often willing to pay higher local taxes if the schools are good, in a sort of virtuous cycle: good schools help their children, and the reputation of these schools also help keep property values high. But what if you don't care about schools? What if you have no children? What if you have one kid and your neighbor has three or six, or a child with special needs such as being born blind or deaf, that result in a higher cost of education? Let's look at one scenario: two homeowners, same district, similar value to the home. Probably pay about the same tax. But one has no children while the other has three. One might argue that the family with children should pay more, or even pay for the cost of their children's education separately. In the abstract that sounds fair. So why don't we do that? Because the overall benefit of universal education is so important that we accept a bit of unfairness for the greater good. That's right, we expect some folks to subsidize others: childless homeowners will find part of their property tax used to send their neighbors' kids to school. Imagine if we suddenly said look, if you can't pay for your kids' education, then don't have any. Or the family with more kids - should we tell them they need to skip even having some of those children? It is not practical - and, importantly, it is just plain hard hearted. And while there may be a touch of unfairness here to the childless, imagine how unfair a world would be where only the well-off could afford to educate their children. Access to a universal education for our children is something we as a nation give ourselves. The decision is ethical and pragmatic, not ideological. I grant that the system is imperfect, and that some people pay more for less, but that is worthwhile in exchange for the overall good.

All that is a rather long-winded way to get to the topic at hand: health care. Like education, it is big, it is complex, it isn't cheap. Some people need a lot of care (just like the family with six kids needing more school dollars) and some people need little to none (the young and the luckily healthy). When you need it, well you need it, but when you don't you don't think much about it - like the childless couple and schools above. But it has an enormous effect both on individuals as well as society as whole. Take our suddenly unemployed breadwinner above - I don't think it's a stretch to imagine that person faced with some tough choices about spending - rent/mortgage, food, utilities, health insurance - what will go?(Just as an aside - the same questions hang over someone starting a business - and thus access to health care can become a barrier for the budding entrepreneur.) As we saw, educating the kids is not a fear. We as a nation have taken that piece of anxiety off the table. Health care is surely as complex as education, and just as crucial to an individual's or family's long-term success. No one can fully predict when illness or an accident may strike. Medical bills can easily explode, and many a family has found itself in bankruptcy thanks to the breadwinner's getting ill or in an accident, becoming unable to work, and then finding the cost of care economically devastating.

Why not complete building a system that has all of us insured? Realistically, we are nearly there. Most working adults have insurance thorough their jobs. Seniors have Medicare. (Which of course takes the most expensive group to insure out of the risk pool.) The poor may qualify for Medicaid. That leaves those working but still can't afford it, and those who might be able to pay, but feel sure they don't need it. Looking around the world, every modern country already has universal coverage. Do they all do it the same way? Of course not: there is a mix of systems, from government run hospitals to single payer to privately run insurance paid for out of taxes, to regulations that simply require everyone to have insurance of some kind. Here in the

U.S. we have the contentious Affordable Care Act, derided as "Obamacare" even though it was based on a Republican think tank derived system implemented in Massachusetts as "Romneycare." Is it a perfect system? Of course not. But, instead of just trashing it, why not fix it? Make it, or okay, something else, work for all of us. (But please, no fake solutions, plans that cover little to nothing, or drop you at the first runny nose.) The problem is we are too stuck in ideologies: "Healthcare is a right!" versus "No to socialized medicine!". At times it seems each side is so intent on demonizing the other, that we don't really focus on the pragmatic aspect. Frankly, in any system someone is going to end up paying for something they don't end up using much of, while someone else is going to get more out of the system than they put in. That's the nature of insurance itself, even if it is all private. Remember the childless couple above? No kids, six kids, same taxes. Unfair in a way, but taking the big picture into account, very fair indeed.

Like education, healthcare is complex and important. And like educating our children, we really all ought to have access to it. How exactly to skin that cat is a tough question, and probably finding our way will require some experimentation. But if we agree on universal access, and the goal of finding a practical way to manage it, then instead of having that uncertainty, we can be free to focus on other, more productive things. Like maybe that new job – or even, if we have the idea – a new business.

6

Gun Control – Or Not? Or Where does Safety Lie?

The American Automobile Association (AAA), in a study about auto safety, estimated that about 8,000 fatalities a year result from accidents involving unlicensed drivers. Kind of gets your hackles up, no? If you have a license to drive a car you bothered to pass a written test, and then, after days and weeks, maybe months of practice, perhaps with a probably stressed out family member, or having paid for lessons, you took the actual on-the-road test, demonstrating you both knew the law and could handle the basic tasks of safety like avoiding pedestrians and making a three point turn. Were you a great driver even then? Unlikely - practice and time are the keys to being able to react quickly, to drive "defensively" and avoid accidents. While there is no current way to make the roads perfectly safe, I'd be surprised if anyone seriously claimed we should just forget the effort and let anyone who pleases behind the wheel. On the other hand, there really are few luddites who recommend we just ban automobiles. No, we try to walk a line between safety and access, and part of that is making sure the operator - the driver - of a car can prove at least some basic knowledge of safe handling.

But you already know I'm not really talking about cars. This is, of course an old argument - we need a license to drive, and need to prove basic skills behind the wheel in order to legally drive - why not demand the same of gun owners? Fact is, many states do, some do not, and over the last decade the law has generally been moving towards less and less regulation, if we take the country as a whole[7]. For driving one hopes that the basic test weeds out someone with no skill at all. But to handle a gun? What would the basic skills be? Is the ability to aim and shoot all that goes into gun safety?

I'm going to start here with a basic premise - I don't want to take guns away from law abiding citizens. Why not? - I believe we should maximize freedom, including allowing others to engage in activities that we may not want to. Don't want a gun - fine, don't buy one. Sure, if every gun in the country were somehow magically banned, then gun shooting deaths would go down. But – it's just as true if every car in the country were banned then there would be an elimination of auto accident fatalities. A bit drastic, no? For many Americans guns are part of important actives for them, legitimate and

---

7   Some gun owners may be surprised by the idea that the law has gotten looser. Check out over the past few decades the number of states that have allowed open carry of a handgun, that beforehand had strict limits on it. Of course, there have been a few states that have tightened up the laws - Connecticut comes to mind. And as a matter of statistics, afterwards the number of gun homicides dropped in that state.

legal, and cause no harm to others. Hitting a target on an afternoon, bringing home game for the table, these are long standing activities that bring people pleasure, and are often handed down by generations. I want to be respected for what I want to do with my leisure time, and therefore should fairly offer the same to others. However - and here is the big caveat - I also expect to be held responsible for what I do, and how my choices impact my neighbors, community and the nation at large.

When we look at the numbers for auto safety, we can see a clear improvement over the years. We've made cars themselves safer (seatbelts, better frames), roads safer, and we've maybe even made us safer (drunk driver laws, weekend stops). Do those things cost money? Sure. Do they mean certain nuisance efforts (everyone loves heading down to the DMV)? Sure. We condemn careless drivers, and rightly so. And while not every rule or regulation is perfect the effort to save lives is worth it.

Can we have a conversation with gun owners to improve matters? For example, every year over 200,000 guns are stolen. The actual number may be even higher, as not every theft is reported, and that number doesn't even include straw purchases. You know the line - if guns were outlawed, only outlaws would have guns? Not exactly - because it looks like outlaws are getting them from legal owners. Where else would they come from - factory direct? When you buy a gun do you have to show how you will keep it secure from theft? How else keep them out of the hands of criminals?

Rather than focus on outlawing guns perhaps we should have an honest conversation about how to keep all of us safe in a world full of guns. Up to now I haven't mentioned the NRA, as frankly just naming the organization can get people hot around the collar, both for and against. But look at the group's roots: in training. They began by helping improve the skills of sharpshooters. and while political advocacy is what most of us know them for, they also hold thousands of training sessions nationwide on safe gun handling. That's right, safe gun handling. What might that look like, if we take into account both owners and those that decline to own?

Did you take drivers ed in high school? Did they show those "horror" movies - crash scenes, stories of frightening trauma and death? Often the warnings were around drinking and driving. They wanted to put the fear in you - to have respect for the fact that barreling down the road in heavy machinery at 60 mph is dangerous. And not just to the driver, but to the innocent who happens to be in front of that machine. Getting a driver's license is for many a rite of passage, a step into adulthood that signals freedom - but profoundly, life and death profoundly, it also means responsibility. Safety training with a gun should not simply include where you point the thing, or how to load a gun, but there is a larger safety, to the public at large. I don't want to own a gun, but I also don't want a stolen gun pointed at my head.

So how would we build a set of responsibilities that still enables gun owners to easily own guns? For starters, how about a rational licensing system? Or keep it state level but mandate some minimums that would go into the license. Background checks would be part of that of course, and while they are not perfect, they could be improved. Then the prospective owner would have to show he or she really has a sense of the risks a gun presented. That is going to mean some honesty about those risks. It has been pointed out that about half of all gun deaths are suicides. Sometimes that is presented as a defense of owner ship - see, that death was no risk to the public at large. As if the person was not a member of the public. Research on suicide shows that the easier a suicide plan is to act on, the more likely someone is to do it[8]. The prospective owner should know that there are times when a gun needs to put away - if you are depressed, or life feels overwhelming, then that is the moment to get help, and crucially, get the gun out of the house.

What about kids? Every year there are toddlers who accidentally shoot themselves, another child or a family member. As a responsible gun owner, you might think what fool left a loaded firearm hanging

---

8   That is why barriers on bridges that make it harder to jump lower the overall suicide rate for the bridge area as a whole, not just the jumpers. If suicide requires a pause to think it through or find a more difficult route, it turns out people are less likely to go through with it.

around, but that is just the point - people do. Was that risk something they were tested on knowing *before* the gun came home? Shouldn't the prospective gun owner have that nightmare on his or her radar? Then there is alcohol. I worked in the restaurant business for many decades, and from the heated arguments I've broken up at the bar on plenty of occasions, I wonder if guns had been around if I would even be typing this.

Let's carry the metaphor of auto license further, to see what steps are involved. Say you have decided to become a gun owner (or are one already). In an effort to improve gun safety, the federal government creates a set of standards for licensing. States would not be required to implement them, but such standards can help set the bar for effective licensing. First, you pass a meaningful background check. This won't catch everything, (incidents without an arrest in your past are likely to be skipped, but that is fair, as we all deserve due process). Then, you review some fundamental aspects of gun safety - and not just handling. That includes the importance of keeping guns stored safely when not in use, out of the hands of minors, and locked up in such a way as to deter theft (do you want to think you kept a gun to keep yourself safe, then find out the gun stolen from your home was used in a homicide? Not your responsibility of course, but it seems fair to ask you to lock up your weapon when not in use.). You will want to be aware of some of the dangers of gun ownership. Remember the drivers' ed courses we talked about with those scary images of car crashes? Was that so you would skip driving? No, just to scare some caution into you. Suicide risk must be covered, as well as the risks to children and household members. If you are buying the gun for self-defense, you should have some training on handling such a situation and recognizing when a gun is not the appropriate answer. You should also learn how to avoid the pitfalls of carrying a gun all the time. Do you really know the statistics on crime?[9] On average, does carrying a gun really make you safer? Or does it just make you feel safer? Think of all the times someone flies off the handle - road rage, bar room arguments, family feuds - if people are carrying guns what would just be an ugly shout fest can turn deadly pretty easily. You may feel you will handle your gun responsibility, but again, we have to take everyone - including the more careless among us - into account. You should also have some hands-on teaching, especially if you are new to handling a gun, and the teacher should check off whether you are safe with the weapon. Finally, you can take a brief written exam, to show you understand these basic safety rules and the risks of gun ownership. And certain things might be fair reasons to lose your rights to ownership - drunk and disorderly while carrying?

---

9   Even the gathering of such statistics is fraught with contention, and a number of groups have tried to suppress honest research in these areas. If you feel responsible enough to own a gun, then it seems fair to ask you to be responsible enough to honestly know the true risks, and to encourage genuine research without a knee jerk reaction to shut such research down.

Spousal abuse with a loaded gun in the house? Due process, sure, but just as we take some folks driver's license away, the same should go with guns. Finally, a system for resale needs to be in place - so that down the road, if you want to sell your weapon (upgrade maybe?) you can be sure the person who buys it is legit.

None of this is harder than getting a driver's license. What might happen, is a few people may decide not to bother. The background check may slow some down. Perhaps gun sales might drop a bit. If that saves lives, isn't it worth it?

One other detail - what kind of gun can you buy? This is a question often raised in connection with mass shootings. Let me pose a scenario to gun owners: you have your weapon with you, you respond to shots and are faced with an active shooter. You get to pick what kind of gun the shooter has: handgun, rifle, or full magazine AR15. How much difference would what kind of gun make? How fast can a person shoot one kind of gun over another, or how often reload with a full magazine. There is a reason some rifles are used in a military context - more firepower, faster shooting, more time before needing to reload. Do you want such weapons to be easily had? If you insist that there is a good, non-military use for this gun (and don't just listen to the boosters, check in with the ex-soldiers who are in favor of banning these type of weapons), then perhaps you might agree that this is not the tool for casual use - could we insist on further background checks along with registration of the each firearm of this type? That way, if you do want to build an arsenal, you might have to come up with a good reason why. I know, no one wants to be on the police's radar, but these kinds of weapons represent some serous firepower - that seems to be the appeal for some - and extra precautions do not seem unfair.

You will notice I have tried to stick to the middle road here: I don't own a gun, but I grew up with guns in the house, and I have no desire to take them away from those citizens who find they are an important part of their lives. Are there people who would like to ban all guns? Sure. But on the other side there are those who think possession of a guns and ammo should be as easy to achieve as buying a quart of milk. Sadly, there are those who take the argument even further, claiming outrageously that mass shootings are a hoax. They have even gone up to the families who have lost loved ones, or children, and called them liars. Picture this: you have lost a child to horror and violence. That alone is unimaginable in its pain. Then you have people saying to your face that the death never happened, you are a liar. This is just vicious. I think the vast majority of gun owners would agree. And just as I would not tar them with the stupidity of the worst extremism on their side, I ask they not assume everyone who wants more gun safety is out to take every gun away. The fact is that much of this could be done by the National Rifle Association right now. If they truly care about their members, don't they want their families to stay safe? One might imagine them discussing suicide risk: perhaps a "buddy" system would help? Gun owners could agree to hold a fellow owner's weapons, "no questions asked." If someone feels overwhelmed by life and finds ending it on his or her mind, the ability to hand over this risk in a safe way would be life empowering. This would even offer an opportunity to reach out with support, an offer to talk, or a non-judgmental hand in friendship. Life can be difficult. Should ending it be easy? Or do we care enough about each other to be willing to support each other through a tough time? Education was once the prime role of the NRA – can they show enough care for their members to have honest discussions around safety, suicide risk, and how to keep one's weapons secure? (Truth is they already do some of this – they offer courses in safe handling and do stress safe storage. But let's also admit that is not always at the top of their agenda.)

I'm going to end with a short scene. A parent, seeing his or her child has "come of age" decides to teach his or her child about guns. They head out to the countryside where the child learns to respect the weapon and handle it safely. There is excitement, but also seriousness. They walk in the fields, moist grasses at their feet, the fresh smell of tress. The hunt is successful, and the child brings home his or her first game birds, ready to be dressed and cooked. Perhaps they said a bit of thanks for the beautiful animal, the colors of plumage, and offer respect for its life and the natural world. Then they sit to a meal that is directly tied to the hunting they did. All over the country there are traditions like this, passed down in families, or from friend to friend. Our efforts to save and protect the natural world bears fruit in such a moment, that in our increasingly urbanized world we are fortunate to have preserved such space in our nation. This is a tradition worthy of respect and preservation. So, let's keep our guns, but find a way to do it more safely.

7

—

An Ancient Debate: Abortion and Choice

Coins from the ancient Greek city of Cyrene on the North African coast were often pressed with an image of the city's primary export: the leaves of the silphium plant, or sometimes of its seed, which was shaped remarkably like a valentine's day heart. The demand for the plant was so great it was harvested to extinction. It had a number of medicinal properties: one of its most notable was as an abortifacient.

Abortion is not new, nor is the debate over it new. Texts from ancient China, Egypt, Rome, Cambodia and other places around the globe discuss a number of ways to terminate a pregnancy, from herbal concoctions to physical acts with sharpened instruments or the application of abdominal pressure. While the bible doesn't mention abortion, it does make a clear distinction between causing a miscarriage, which would have been punished by a fine, with the taking of human life, a capital crime. In the Talmud a fetus is often described as a "part" of the mother, particularly before 40 days post conception. Early Catholicism has vacillated over the centuries, the argument frequently focusing on when the soul enters the fetus: some authors believed at conception, but others described it as occurring at "quickening" the stage during pregnancy when a woman first senses fetal movement, at around 15 to 17 weeks. Within Protestant denominations there is a range of stances, from fiercely against it, to others that support the idea of it being a matter of individual choice. Muslim stances also vary, with greater restrictions among conservative groups. Just by looking at these major Western religions we can see that there has been a broad range of historical positions that vary over time and denomination.

In the last chapter we discussed gun control, and one of the crucial aspects of that debate is over respecting someone's choice to do things that you yourself might find undesirable. You may not want to own a gun, but does that make it appropriate to outlaw guns for those that do? There is little risk in our society from a careful and well-trained gun owner, who keeps his or her weapons secure from theft and knows there are inappropriate times for guns to be around. In a free country there is a delicate balance between different peoples' desires; and one should hesitate before curtailing others' choices.

Let's look at some of the more commonly cited reasons to ban abortion, as well as the logic of allowing the procedure to remain legal. Religion frequently plays a central role, and those with strong faith often make up the ranks of those trying hardest to make it illegal. As we saw in the first chapter on the place of faith in a democracy, that is a problem. If you recall, we looked at the story of Abraham and Isaac. Just as Isaac must have a say in his own fate, regardless of his father's belief, so to we cannot in good conscience make a law based on any one particular faith alone. Your faith may tell you that abortion is wrong - and if you wish to remain true to your faith, then you might safely not have one. But to compel others to live by the rules of that faith is to violate their right to live within the rules of their own faith, or even none at all. This is not to say those of faith may not seek to persuade others or vote in accord with their conscience (lawmakers however, in their oath to uphold the constitution, should not seek to enforce the dictates of any particular faith). Faith alone is simply an inappropriate basis for the law. If faith were, we would be living in a Theocracy, where the religious authorities are the ultimate arbiter of the law. We rightfully condemn such societies as lacking in some of the most basic human freedoms. Therefore, religious creeds are not a good reason to ban abortion.

The health of the mother is often cited as another reason. If we look honestly at the data, it seems clear that early abortion is significantly safer than carrying a child to term. As for psychological harm, no genuine study has shown any at all, and while it is important to note that some woman may regret having an abortion, we do not routinely ban choices on the basis that some citizen may have regrets. And absent really compelling evidence, don't we get to make choices for ourselves that we may feel are difficult and raise some self-doubt, without the law interfering with our choice?

Of course, the most contentious arguments concern the status of the fetus itself. For some the moment of conception is the start of a new person, and any interference in that is murder. But does that honestly capture the nature of pregnancy?

Pregnancy is a both a path and a process. Every month, generally, a woman of childbearing age will release a single egg from her ovaries (with some exceptions, for example sometimes two eggs are released, with a potential for fraternal twins). The average male's body creates 1500 sperm cells a second (!) or around 290 million a day. Yet the reality is the vast majority of both sperm and eggs will never end up as part of a new person. Here we have the first stage - the body's creation of sperm and egg. Each egg and sperm cell do have at least the potential to combine, but we do not mourn the loss of either. Even after they combine, many, if not most will never continue to term. It is estimated that as much as 75 percent of fertilized eggs fail to implant in the uterine wall, and as many as a third of those implanted will fail to be viable, often due to genetic abnormalities. Most of these a woman will not even be aware of and will be expelled during menstruation. She may even note her period is late and then resumes – at times this could be the loss of a fertilized egg. We may treat conception as the beginning of personhood, but clearly nature does not.

At 12 weeks - three months, the proverbial first

trimester - the fetus weighs half an ounce, or less than the weight of three quarters. Why not right now get three quarters and hold them in your hand? That small weight is greater than the fetus at that stage. But with the hard work of the pregnant woman's body, through the interface of the placenta, the dual blood supplies will meet and trade nutrients and waste, to help the fetus develop and grow. This singular road, the unique genetic combination, this particular person, may then come to be. What if a woman decides at this point that she is not ready? Perhaps she already has children, and a family, and the additional resources of time and money on another child will tax her ability to fully care for what she has? Or maybe she is young, and has life plans that take all her effort, the energy to finish school, get a job, establish herself financially and personally, before having a child? It is true that to end a pregnancy would end something unique - this egg and this sperm will not come together again in this combination, and so this particular path will be gone forever. But then, later, other combinations will be possible, perhaps this time a wanted pregnancy, also an utterly singular combination of genes, that may be joyfully nurtured by the woman's body, a road that leads to a child, a road that, had the earlier combination not been aborted, might never have been taken, and this, equally unique mix of genes, would never exist had the earlier pregnancy been maintained. Every choice opens some possibilities while leaving others behind.

Clearly there are a number of points where this process - pregnancy - might be interrupted. Contraception is of course a big one - to prevent sperm and egg from combining, or the new combination from attaching to the uterine wall and beginning the process of growing a placenta. It is at that first stage that laws have been passed to stop people from affecting the process. In the U.S. many of these have been called Comstock laws and were enacted in the late 1800's. For us today the notion that the government has attempted to reach into our most private activities - in the bedroom! - seems intrusive to say the least. Granted, for some the notion of sex without the immediate goal of reproduction is wrong in itself. Yet do we really want the mechanism of the state - even legitimately elected by the majority - to control this choice?

At what point can we clearly say there is a separate individual there? At what point can we interfere? In the 1965 Supreme Court decision Griswold vs Connecticut the old Comstock laws against contraception were found to be unconstitutional. And that decision, less contentious today, stands as an important basis for the later, much more controversial one: Roe vs. Wade.

One of the most argued aspects of Roe vs Wade was the claim of a right to privacy - that the constitution limits government interference in our private lives. That seems reasonable: do you believe the government should stick its nose into ANY aspect of your life without some compelling public reason? In Griswold, the topic was contraception - do you want the government telling you and your partner that you cannot use birth control? Some religious faiths are against contraception, but do we allow them to tell everyone how to make that choice? The right to decide for ourselves on such private matters seems a fundamental aspect of a free society.

If we look honestly at pregnancy, I think we see a process - from sperm and egg, insemination, implanting - with many stages. Preventing the very beginning of that process – contraception – no longer seems very contentious. And at that end of that process, with childbirth, there is indisputably a separate person, with all the rights of personhood. At the beginning? It feels false to call a single fertilized cell a person. I think for most Americans there is an intuitive sense of this reality - ending a pregnancy early is a personal decision that says I do not want to continue on this road, ending a pregnancy very late is more wrenching, with a sense that there is a genuine human life at stake[10]. Somewhere, along the path, there is another life that we can argue to protect. That exact moment can be argued - four months?

---

10   This is of course a dilemma that others have taken up - an example would be maternal risk, in which a pregnant woman would have to risk her life to carry the child to term. Imagine a mother, say with a family, several children, a spouse, who finds herself facing that risk. What of the children she already has - should they risk losing a mother over her pregnancy? However you feel about abortion, do you really think this sort of intensely personal private decision should be made by the government? One might fairly regulate late term abortion (by delineating reasonable parameters), but at heart this too is a tough choice that seems best made by a woman and her physician.

Six? But at the end of the day, it is the pregnant woman who bears the burden of pregnancy; it is her body, and if each of our bodies isn't something we can demand the government keep its hands off of, then what is?

8

—

Does Anybody Really Like
Affirmative Action?

For this chapter you'll have to do a bit of homework. Before reading further, get online and do a search for "lynching postcards." There will be more than one site, take your time and look through a few of them. It'll probably be difficult to tear your eyes from the mangled bodies of the victims, but many of the images also show crowds, and if so, scan through them at the faces. Keep in mind these aren't just news photos - they were often taken by a local photographer who turned them into postcards. Members of the crowd would purchase and send them to friends and family. Inscriptions on the back often include bragging about the person's role in the lynching. As you look at the crowds, you may be struck by how ordinary those folks seem - these are the same faces you might see in an image illustrating life on Main Street USA. Now remember that over seventy percent of lynching in the United States was of African Americans. Nor is this ancient history - begun after the civil war, it continued through the twentieth century, the 1930's, 40's 50's and even the 60's. Keep those images in your mind, both victims and crowds.

Part two of your homework: look up redlining and home buying, particularly in the post-World War II period. Redlining segregated certain neighborhoods off from others, particularly African American communities, as too risky for banks to offer mortgages too, or to offer them only at inflated rates. The name came from the practice of outlining areas on a map; many of such maps were created by the federal government, although private businesses such as banks made their own versions. This was combined with well documented lending patterns that might offer loans to much poorer or less financially qualified whites, while denying them to better qualified African Americans. The practice was widespread, with support of institutions in government and banking. The clear effect was to keep African American's from getting a mortgage, regardless of their ability to pay. It has often been said that homeownership is one of the essential keys to upward mobility. The expansion of the middle class in the US after the War closely parallels the growth in homeownership. Yet this crucial part of economic success was denied to most African Americans.

Keep these two things in mind - the terror of lynching and being blocked from access to a critical part of financial security.

Now I want you to try a little thought experiment. Imagine you are in charge of hiring for your firm, and let's also imagine it is at least a mid-size company with a few hundred employees. On your desk there is a stack of resumes, and your first task is to winnow that pile down to a few promising candidates that you will call in for an interview. Perhaps their photos are attached. Certainly, there are names. But are those factors relevant? Surely you are looking for other things: work experience for the job, good references, in the case of a recent graduate, perhaps grades and academic honors. You may look at outside interests - someone who volunteers in the community might be a good representative for your company. Surely one thing you think you are not going to let be a factor is race. Perhaps not consciously - but - multiple studies have shown that resumes that include clues that the person applying for the job is a member of a minority are less likely to get a call back. A number of versions of the study have been done: some with more African American sounding names, some with photographs of the applicant, some that show outside interests associated with African Americans. Over and over such resumes resulted in lower call back rates. In fact, some African - Americans have taken to "whitening" their resume, to increase their odds of getting that crucial chance at an interview.

What did we get out of our quick homework assignment? We began with a vivid reminder of the brutality and violence African Americans have received in our country. And images that show that the perpetrators aren't some crazed outlying group of fanatics, but that they are us, straight out of main street. Then we saw how our institutions worked to create powerful barriers such as redlining to prevent African Americans from economic success. Finally, we saw how race still plays a profound role even with a simple (but critical) process such as winnowing down a stack of resumes. We have historical terrorism that continued well into the 20th century, institutional racism that damaged a chance at economic success, a current state of bias (often unconscious) that erects barriers to opportunity.

And oh, we haven't mentioned slavery. Or a century of segregation. Spend a bit of time researching the issue and it's hard to imagine someone arguing that African Americans have gotten, or are getting now, a fair deal.

So, how should we respond? Ignore? Pretend that the "bad stuff" only happened in the past? There has been one attempt at an answer: Affirmative Action. Two dirty words, to many. Who likes it? I doubt if anyone does. No one likes to think he or she was beaten out - or chosen! - over skin color. One person feels cheated, the other his or her accomplishments demeaned. It seems to fly against our stated national goal of equality, where the color of one's skin plays no role in how someone is judged. But, as we have seen, the color of one's skin indeed does play a role - a powerful, soul crushing role, if we are honest. Should we act as if our ideal has already been achieved?

The argument over affirmative action often plays out in the world of college admissions. Recognizing how widespread our biases are - remember, even an African

American sounding name can change how a resume is evaluated - college admission boards can try to circumvent this bias by seeking a diverse student body. Guess what happens? Sometimes an African American with a lower GPA gets in ahead of a white person with a higher GPA. Numerous lawsuits have of course been filed by students who have been denied admission to their college choice, beaten out by a black student with lower grades. Easy to understand their frustration: we live in hyper-competitive times, and a hardworking student is going to feel they should have gotten in on merit alone.[11] The answer then comes back that the bias - or outright racism - that blacks have suffered is simply being partially ameliorated, and that whiteness itself is a kind of privilege. Can you see where this is going? Another attempt to solve an injustice can cause side effects that appear unjust as well.

Remember in the chapter on health care we discussed how a basically good social policy - universal education - can have an unfair aspect, in that those without children end up subsidizing the education of those that do. Perhaps that is one way to view Affirmative Action, as an overall sensible policy that sometimes results in less than desirable outcomes. Affirmative action is an attempt to recognize our own weaknesses, to say we can't just look away like children and expect

---

11   Funny that legacy admissions – students accepted because their parents went to that same school – doesn't raise as many hackles.

the world to fix itself.

Perhaps though, there is another choice. Can we build a world where affirmative action isn't needed? That is the ideal, isn't it? How would we get there? Frankly, much of the job is going to fall on white Americans, because any real appraisal of history and our current state is going to show we built this world, and it's our attitudes that need to change. Can we begin with a little honesty, both about our nation's history, as well as its current state? And what about listening, rather than reacting. When African Americans' talk about the school to prison pipeline, or bias in hiring, or Black Lives Matter, try not to answer with a shout that "White Lives Matter too!" as if African Americans' desire to have a fair place at the table is some kind of "reverse racism." When things are unjust, a call for justice is simply that - a call for a better, fairer world.

And oh, none of this will be easy. But the easy things, really, are they what we are most proud of?

One more thing - go back and give those lynching postcards one more look. This is us. Is it who we want to be?

9

—

What is Right? What is Law?
The Death Penalty

In the 1988 presidential debate between George H. Bush and Michael Dukakis, the moderator, Bernard Shaw, asked Dukakis a question that many see as one of the more damaging moments during his campaign. It was a hypothetical question, designed to pin him down: would he support the death penalty for someone proven guilty of raping and murdering his wife Kitty. He answered in a measured, calm ,fashion, reiterating his opposition to the death penalty, and went on the clarify that the death penalty has no deterrent effect on crime, and in fact during his tenure as governor of Massachusetts he had successfully lowered overall crime rates by more humane methods. In the end he looked cold and false, attached to an abstract principal over the safety of his family. Yet, was he right?

In the well-known story of Cain and Abel the bible tells the story of the "first" murder. Cain's motive is largely seen to be that of jealous rage over God's preference for Abel's sacrificial offering over his own, although some traditions have held that there was a conflict over who each would marry. What is not in question is Cain's guilt: the God of the Bible is omnipotent, and when he confronts Cain there is no doubt who has committed the crime. It is also clear that God might easily have killed Cain as punishment in turn. Yet he does not - instead he has Cain live for eternity, with the crime hanging over him, wandering the earth as an outcast from society.

I do not bring up this story to say it should be a template for our modern laws. Rather the tale shows us something of motive, and irrational motive at that. Why wouldn't Cain have tried first to offer another sacrifice - in other words, just get that right? Why not turn to his brother and ask for help? And surely Cain must have known that God, in his infinite knowledge, would know of his guilt. Murder, as portrayed here, is an irrational act. The law, however, must be based on reason. Not that we ignore how irrational human beings act. Rather we should carefully weigh how we punish.

From that perspective, Dukakis was citing the truth, that there is no evidence that the death penalty has a deterrent effect on violent crime[12]. He was refusing to personalize a public policy, or engage, however

---

12   It should be noted that it may have a deterrent effect on freedom, in those societies with absolutist governments. If calm headed, reason-based acts, such as speaking out against the regime, are punished by death that may indeed fulfill the regimes wishes. Thus we have a paradox - the death penalty, supposedly enforced by calm and measured rules, only functions as a deterrent against reasonable behavior such as free thought and expression. It is not likely to deter people who are acting irrationally, like a criminal after gain, or someone in a rage, or psychologically disturbed, or indeed seeking personal vengeance.

hypothetically, with the emotion of a victim to how the law should be constructed. That seems sensible, but he neglected a central aspect of punishment. Personal feelings are enormously important to the victims of a crime. I can see no way to judge someone, who, having lost a loved one, desires that the perpetrator die as well. Some have said this provides closure and peace - others feel that it is merely a form of revenge and that forgiveness is the only genuine way to find comfort. There are certainly stories of families, who, having lost a loved one to a senseless crime, find some measure of comfort and long-term peace in forgiveness. Yet I cannot see any real way to consistently measure that - perhaps both are true and depend on the nature of the survivors as well as the circumstances of the crime. Certainly, we have all read of horrific crimes where there does not seem to be any punishment severe enough to be called a just response. Frankly, facing the same question that Dukakis did, I do not know what my feelings would be. Perhaps I too would want to see the murderer killed, perhaps even by my own hands. Not that I am advocating for a revenge-based society - but I think it is dishonest to pretend that human beings never hunger for that.

But the death penalty is not merely an act rising from pain and vengeance. It is a public policy, a law, a supposedly cool-headed response to an unmeasurably disturbing act. It takes a trial, a judge, a jury, a public to support it, a public in whose name the sentence will be imposed and then carried out. Every step must be perfect. Remember the old adage, better ten guilty men go free, rather than a single innocent man be punished? Now imagine the stakes are the ultimate ones, of life and death. Now imagine someone must push that button in the end, throw some switch. What if we get it wrong and an innocent man is executed?

The Innocence Project was begun over 25 years ago, with a simple mission: utilize DNA evidence to help prisoners who have been wrongly convicted. Since then hundreds have been set free. These are people who spent an average of 14 years in jail for a crime he or she did not commit. Let's get that clear: these are prisoners who were convicted and sentenced, having gone through our criminal justice system, with the full safeguards of judge and jury. Yet the system got it wrong, horribly so. The project has also helped identify over 150 actual assailants – the real guilty parties. This is not about finding "technicalities" to undermine a prosecution, such as one might see on a TV show: this about setting the innocent free. I would urge you to visit the Innocence Project's web site, where you'll find eye opening stories of individual cases, as well as disturbing statistics that demonstrate some of the errors that went into the conviction of the innocent. Does that mean we should give up charging people with a crime? Of course not. But the frightening implication is that there is a very real probability that somewhere along the line we have executed an innocent man.

Now let that sink in for a moment. Imagine you, or someone you love, executed for a crime he or she did not commit.

Victims, and the families and friends, neighbors and communities of victims, all deserve to be heard. But our institutions are based on human skill and human assessment, and as such are imperfect and likely to remain so despite our best efforts. We may feel we have certainty - even a confession[13] - but then the evidence shows how often we get it wrong. I do not know how I would deal with such a terrible loss as that of the senseless death of a loved one, nor can I say with any clarity what a just punishment would be for some of the horrific crimes we have all seen over the years. But to coolly put someone to death, in this structured institutional manner does not seem to be just. In the story of the first murder, death was not met with death, but with endless time to comprehend being cast out. God, omnipotent, by definition unable to be fooled by the evidence, did not chose to meet death with death. So again, when the time for us to set punishment arrives: what if we get it wrong?

---

13 Approximately 1 out of 4 of those exonerated by DNA evidence with The Innocence Project gave a false confession. Why or how that occurs is reviewed on the web site in detail, but again this is a number that should give us pause.

10

The Newcomers, or How Open Should the Door be For Immigration?

In the year 1492, a sailor on board a small ship cried out that he had seen land. The leader of that expedition was of course Christopher Columbus. Coming on shore to one of the Caribbean islands of what are now called the Bahamas, he and his men found natives who welcomed them with food and gifts, and eagerly traded for the beads and trinkets he had. The beginning of the European conquest of the Americas had begun.

As we know, it did not turn out to be a good deal for the Native Americans. Columbus wrote in his log that this first group of natives bore no arms, and that with fifty men he could subjugate them all. Over the course of four journeys, Columbus kidnapped and enslaved many natives, forcing them to work as guides and bringing others back to Europe. Many died on the way. Motivated by greed and the search for profit, he had noticed the gold earrings worn by the natives, and he became relentless in a search for the source of the metal. On Haiti, where he imagined there were large hidden gold fields, he forced the natives to bring back quotas of gold flakes from the local streams. Those unable to find enough had their hands cut off.

It is not easy to accept that one of the foundational heroes of the Americas wrecked so much pain and havoc on the native population. One is tempted to try to explain it in the context of the times or justify it as the bringing of Christianity or Civilization. As a child that was much of the way that history was taught to me, but of course now we know more, and see that often enough there is more than one perspective to evaluating a hero. I think it pays to understand this complexity, partly to recognize the truth of our own history, and partly as a warning to behave in a just and decent manner moving forward. Looked at from the perspective of the Native Americans (who of course had their own names for themselves) the coming of Columbus was a disaster. With hindsight, and had they had the power to do so, might they have built a giant barrier to keep the Europeans out?

The fear of newcomers is not new in American History, (nor any nation's history). If the historical foundation of the settlement of the America's is one of brutality and the supplanting of the native population, is it any wonder we are suspicious of new arrivals? Our ancestors brought pain, disease, and displacement. If we open our doors today what will newcomers bring to us? Crime? Competition? New languages, new foods, new faiths? Will they assimilate? Will they gather in their own clans, and undermine the cohesiveness of our communities? Or will they become the most grateful of Americans, eager to become part of our grand and ongoing experiment, new champions of freedom, hardworking, friendly, ready to give of themselves for the chance to be part of our story?

Maybe the honest answer is yes - both the good and the bad. What they will be, for sure, is human - and that means some will astound us with their patient, hardworking, responsible selves and some will annoy us, and some will go on to commit crimes that will horrify and cause our tribal selves to rise up and blame the whole group, whatever group that happens to be at any given time, whether Mexican or Muslim now or Chinese or Southern and Eastern European in the past.

Let's look at another historical migration, but this time of Americans settling into what was at the time, another country: the settling of Texas, then part of Mexico.

In 1821 Mexico won its independence from Spain. Texas was at part of that new nation, on land that had been first visited by conquistadores in 1519 and had been argued over by primarily the French and Spanish (of course there were Native Americans there as well). The land that is now Texas was sparsely settled, and the new government of Mexico encouraged immigration; Americans as well as Germans began to move in, and by 1834 the population of Anglos had reached over 30,000, far more than the 8,000 or so Mexicans. Naturally this set the stage for conflict, and eventually the Americans sought independence from the Mexican Government.

A series of violent fights ensued; in 1845 Texas joined the United States, War with Mexico ensued and by 1848 after their defeat the Mexican government was forced to formally recognize Texas as part of the U.S. (as wells as other territory that would become all or part of California, Arizona, Utah, Colorado, Nevada and Southern Wyoming).

This is, of course, just a quick summary; the full details are an important aspect of American and New World History, and well worth looking up, especially as to how the territory played out in terms of the debate over slavery. But clearly this is another example of large-scale immigration playing out very poorly to local people, in this case the Mexican nationals. So again, isn't it reasonable to fear immigration?

This is precisely the question being asked by a number of far-right European Political parties. Some have begun to use an image of Sitting Bull, and warned that the people of Germany or Italy could end up living on reservations if immigration continues unchecked.

A closer look does show some patterns. Columbus brought with him a far more technologically advanced civilization, as well as a claimed moral backdrop for conquest (spreading Christianity) and a frank determination to economically exploit the new world for profit. Combined with successive waves of Europeans and the spread of new diseases that the native populations had little to no resistance for, it meant the doom of their civilizations. In Texas, again the numbers were overwhelming, and combined with the power of the United States and the instability of the relatively new Mexican government, the territory was overwhelmed and taken. Enormous numbers, technological superiority, are all good reasons to fear immigration. But is that what we are facing today?

Or are we seeing people who want to become a part of what we are, not to supplant, but to join and contribute? Groups that now think of themselves as utterly American can look back and often see their ancestors viewed as threats to the American way of life. Historically, Christians have been suspicious of Jews, Protestants of Catholics, northern Anglo Saxon Europeans suspicious of Eastern and Southern Europeans. Italians, Asians, Latin Americans, each has been broadly characterized as "different" in some fundamental way that would prevent them from becoming true Americans. Over and over we have attributed to incoming groups a "less than human" nature. And yet we have seen, that although it may take a generation or two, or even three, that people do assimilate, and become productive and patriotic Americans. But - do they erase their own past, their language, their food, the surface aspects of their culture? No, they bring those things and in time they become parts of all of us, enriching our way of life, from what we eat to how we understand the world, while becoming essentially American in ideal and act.

What is unfortunate is how this debate is so hotly politicized. What would a practical approach look like? It would center on human decency and fairness, and include economics, jobs, opportunity and impact for native and immigrant alike. To have control of our borders is a sensible goal, and to consciously determine who does and does not enter seems reasonable. And having employers verify who they hire would help ensure that work is done legally (the current system is only spottily enforced). Yet would we want to become people who shut the door forever? Think of two perspectives: the farmer who needs seasonal, often migratory labor to pick crops - for him or her the presence of immigrants is a necessity for his business, as the labor he needs changes with the seasons and does not provide much in the way of stability, jobs that more established citizens rarely if ever want. That says we need immigrants. Then think of the worker who hangs sheetrock in the building trade in Southern California - isn't it likely he might see a better wage if there were a shortage of people to do the job? That perspective says we need less. How to balance? What is best for our overall economy, and, taking care of the whole, do we keep in mind how each of us is affected? These are practical considerations, and worthy of debate. But they do not justify demonizing immigrants or turning our backs on fellow humans who are fleeing violence and unrest, or hating those who dream of being part of this country, who seek opportunity and offer hard work in return.

Of course, there is still an elephant in the room:

those who are currently here illegally. Many have spent years building lives, good lives of responsibility, of work, family and community. Many came out of hope and dreams of a better life. In some ways we have left them hanging, as their limbo has meant they provide a ready pool of labor that at times an employer might prefer: their illegal status means the boss need not feel pressured to respect the same legal responsibilities he or she might feel obligated to offer a U.S. citizen. As we have fought over this battle for decades, we have left millions with insecure futures, often assimilated in act and deed, but legally in jeopardy. Is that a just choice?

What seems clear is that we are talking about fellow human beings. Imperfect, like we all are. Certainly, vet people who want to come here, certainly, control how many to a manageable number. Take a practical approach that respects the needs of business as well as the job markets of current citizens, and the ability of communities to assimilate newcomers (a big city and a small town are going to be impacted very differently). We are not talking about the massive numbers that took over Texas, or the technologically advanced Europeans who overran the Native Americans. Those are cautionary tales, but that is not what we face, in spite of political parties that want to exploit our insecurities. It feels fair, and part of the essential nature of the U.S. to honor our own ancestors, who so often came here pursuing dreams of prosperity and freedom, and who we owe a debt of gratitude for the advantages we now have. They were human, just as the stranger at our doors today are human. Take a good look; todays stranger can be tomorrows valued neighbor, grateful and dreaming, like us, of a shared future.

Afterward

Take a Breath: Listen and then Talk

There is a reason we ended with immigration. It is the root, the basis of our nation, the place nearly all of us have come from, and the defining factor of our history. Even if your family floated over on the Mayflower or jumped ship from one of Columbus' famous first three, that is still only a few hundred years, a tiny slice of time compared to the thousands of recorded human history. Our nation, is, well, young. Perhaps that is why, at times we feel unsettled, ever seeking our place and the right way to be.

There are still Native Americans here. Of course, you say, but it is easy to forget. Herded into reservations, their cultures battered, their land taken, they pop up as diminished mascots as we tuck them away from our daily concerns. That is part of us too. Like slavery and post-Civil War Jim Crow, like the so many "little" wars of aggression that we so easily forget. Have you, as a person, lived a perfect, blameless life? (not me). Is not honesty of your flaws the first step in overcoming them? Thinking you are perfect means you never will be. This moment we live in grew out of our past, the moments before flowing like a train rolling down a mountainside, the force of gravity alone to make it fly. Will we just ride it? Or, will we take hold of the controls and steer to the green valleys that await?

To be honest, there is no certain path, no sure way to be. And that is the essential genius of America: we, or our ancestors, came from somewhere else, from everywhere else, from all over the globe. We brought our perspectives, languages, culture, history. All to be part of a new story, one of freedom and opportunity, for ourselves, for our children.

As a young boy, I had heard that if everyone would say the rosary every day the world would be granted peace. I did my bit, sincere in hope and the faith I had learned. Still, the wars raged on. One might call my faith silly, or naïve. In a way, it was. For it was not the form of the prayer – the rosary just happened to be what I grew up with – but the content of the hope, and the way one embodied it in one's life that is the real point. For the prayer for peace can only succeed when it is a grounding for how we approach others: with open hearts and hands. As different as they may be.

It is unlikely that we will ever agree on all the issues that confront us. That does not mean we cannot seek, and find, common solutions. There is a hunger, across the nation, for the endless rage of our entrenched positions to dissipate. For practical solutions to come to the fore. That will not be easy; we are out of practice, inflamed and raw. Remember that the billionaire and the janitor who cleans his office are both stakeholders in our communities. Both deserve a fair seat at the table. The solutions that a large city needs are not exactly the same as a rural mining town. But then – decent jobs, a home one can afford, clean water and good schools, enough money for the doctor and the kids' college, time with one's friends and loved ones – doesn't that sound like a list that *any* community might want for all its citizens?

We have inherited a vast nation, a world military and economic power, yes, but also the shinning place on the hill, the place of dreams, for freedom, for opportunity, the place to be who one is, fully, and still have a place at the table to succeed for oneself and one's children. Let's listen to each other and recognize our common humanity. And continue to build this dream forward.